In Level 0, **Step 1** is ideal fc
beginning their synthetic p
letter sounds introduced in

s a t p i n m c

Special features:

Read this introduction to your child

Captain Comet has arrived on the Pirate Planet.
Look at all the objects that begin with the letter sound p.
What does Pirate Pop have for the party?

popcorn

p

pumpkin

pencil

pizza

penguins

12

plane

polar bear

pillow

potatoes

parrot

presents

peas

Pirate Pop

13

Initial letter sound is in large, clear type

Captain Comet is searching for Marvin the magician.
Look at all the marvellous objects that begin with the letter sound m and help Captain Comet find him.

map

m

magnet

monkey

mermaid

moon

melon

Marvin the magician

moose

meteor

motorbike

mammoth

18

mouse

19

Pictures and labels help children practise the initial letter sound

Phonics and Book Banding Consultant: Kate Ruttle

LADYBIRD BOOKS

UK | USA | Canada | Ireland | Australia
India | New Zealand | South Africa

Ladybird Books is part of the Penguin Random House group of companies
whose addresses can be found at global.penguinrandomhouse.com.

www.penguin.co.uk   www.puffin.co.uk   www.ladybird.co.uk

A version of this book was previously published as
Captain Comet's Space Party – Ladybird I'm Ready for Phonics: Level 1, 2014
This edition published 2018
007

A CIP catalogue record for this book is available from the British Library

ISBN: 978-0-241-31245-2

All correspondence to
Ladybird Books
Penguin Random House Children's
One Embassy Gardens, 8 Viaduct Gardens, London SW11 7BW

Space Party

Written by Catherine Baker
Illustrated by Ian Cunliffe

Captain Comet is having a party. Look at the objects that begin with the letter sound s.

Can you find two super party snacks?

snail

stars

sweets

starfish

stairs

seahorse

6

seal

saxophone

spider

sock

snake

sandwiches

Spaceman Sam

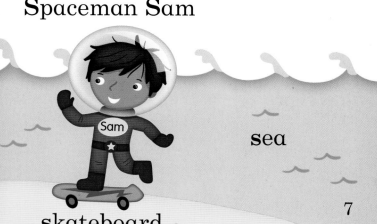

sea

skateboard

7

Captain Comet is zooming
through Asteroid Alley.
Look at the objects that begin
with the letter sound a.

Can you spot an astronaut
to invite to the party?

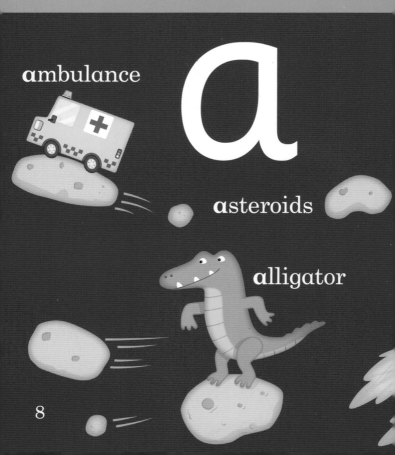

ambulance

a

asteroids

alligator

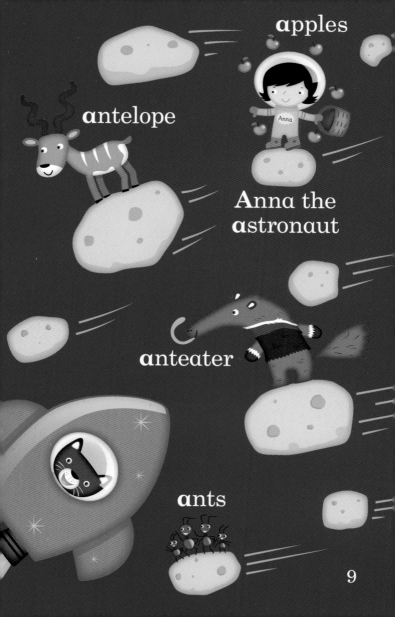

apples

antelope

Anna the
astronaut

anteater

ants

9

Captain Comet needs to find a party prize. Look at all the objects that begin with the letter sound t.

What would you choose?

toad

t

teddy

train

tiger

tea

teapot

turtle

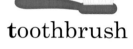

toothbrush

television

toothpaste

toast

tractor

toaster

Captain Comet has arrived
on the Pirate Planet.
Look at all the objects that
begin with the letter sound **p**.

What does Pirate Pop have
for the party?

popcorn

pumpkin

pencil

pizza

penguins

12

plane

polar bear

pillow

potatoes

parrot

presents

peas

Pirate Pop

13

Captain Comet is visiting Planet Impossible. He has lost his party invitations!

Look at all the objects that begin with the letter sound **i**, and help him find them.

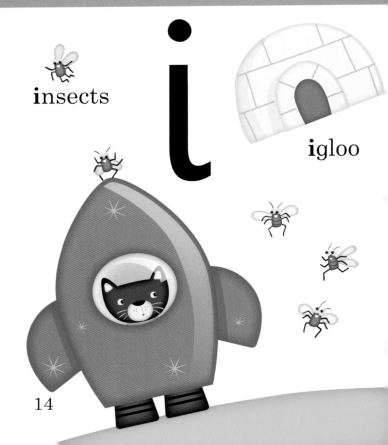

insects

i

igloo

14

ink

invitations

ink pot

iguana

15

Captain Comet has landed on Planet Neptune. He invites his friend Nat to the party.

What else can you see that begins with the letter sound n?

napkin

n

nuts

newt

neighbours

needle

newspaper

notebook

nest

Nat

net

Captain Comet is searching for Marvin the magician.

Look at all the marvellous objects that begin with the letter sound **m** and help Captain Comet find him.

m

map

magnet

meteor

moose

monkey

mermaid

moon

melon

Marvin the **m**agician

motorbike

mouse

mammoth

19

On Planet Dopple, Captain Comet invites his friend Dot to the party.

Look at all the objects that begin with the letter sound **d**, and see if you can spot dancing Dot.

dart

d

donkey

dog

Dot

20

dragon

doughnuts

door

dice

drumsticks

dinosaur

drum

ducks

Guess what colour everything is on Planet Orange? Look at the objects that begin with the letter sound **o**.

What party drink is Otto the octopus holding?

oranges

O

olive

ox

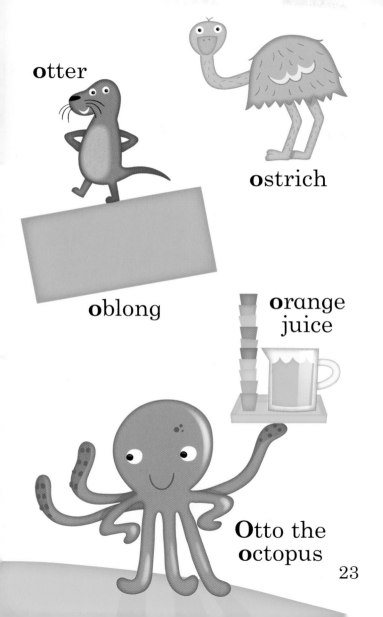

otter

ostrich

oblong

orange juice

Otto the **o**ctopus

23

Cosmic Caroline is cooking some party food. Look at the objects that begin with the letter sound **c**.

Can you find two cool party treats?

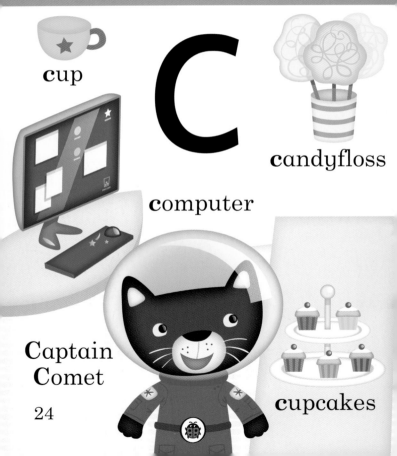

cup

C

candyfloss

computer

Captain Comet

24

cupcakes

cobweb

camel

castle

car

carrots

cauldron

Cosmic
Caroline

25

On Planet Rollercoaster, Rusty the robot races past Captain Comet. He doesn't want to be late for the party.

What other objects can you see that begin with the letter sound r?

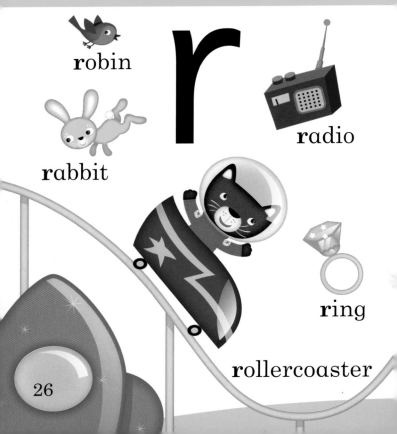

robin

r

radio

rabbit

ring

rollercoaster

rocket

rain

raccoon

Rusty
the
robot

ruler

river   **r**at

27

Captain Comet's friend Big Bear Bill lives on Planet Boomerang. He's got the best bits for the party.

What can you see that begins with the letter sound **b**?

ball

bus

bee

boomerang

beaver

biscuits

28

bats

boat

bread

balloon

banana

bird

butterfly

Big Bear
Bill

29

All the friends have arrived on Planet Fun. It's time for the fancy-dress party to begin!

What costumes can you see that start with the letter sound f?

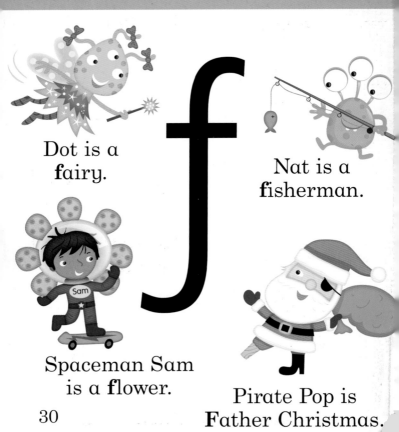

Dot is a **f**airy.

Nat is a **f**isherman.

Spaceman Sam is a **f**lower.

Pirate Pop is **F**ather Christmas.

30